The London Experiment – An Econometric Approach to Assessing Foreign Direct Investment

By Sebastian Meyer

Digital Edition

Copyright © 2013 Sebastian Meyer

All Rights Reserved

Table of Contents

I. Research Problem and Methodology 1

II. A Theoretical Framework of FDI 3

    1.) FDI from a Macro Perspective 3

    2.) FDI from a Micro Perspective 4

    3.) A Technical Model of FDI 5

III. Conclusion and outlook 14

VI. Appendix 15

V. References 49

I. Research Problem and Methodology

The research question of this term paper is to prove the hypothesis of Bradley and Fitzgerald (1990) that '' *[an] analysis of FDI [consists of] necessary component[s] of the integration of [...] multinational enterprises [...]* ''. The aim is to firstly specify, estimate and eventually evaluate a technical model of Foreign Direct Investment (FDI) inflows to the United Kingdom (UK) on the example of the financial service field in London between 1985 and 2010. In doing so, this research problem is approached in an incremental and deductive way because the theoretical research findings are empirically applied to the financial service area in London. First of all, the paper justifies the relevance and international trends of FDI globally and for the UK. The next section shifts from a macro to micro perspective where the focus lies on FDI inflows to the financial service sector in London. In this regard, some exemplary and specific determinants of FDI are assessed through the lenses of an econometric model. Ultimately, based on the correct technical model, a possible outlook is given in order to emphasize some expectations for the future development.

II. A Theoretical Framework of FDI

1.) FDI from a Macro Perspective

Figure 1 illustrates that FDI transactions have increasingly become a significant topic in global world statistics. Within the last three decades, there was a total FDI upwards trend by more than 1000%. Furthermore, FDI inflows increased by about one percent to nearly $ 1.5 trillion. Compared to the boom in 2007, the development of FDI has not recovered yet from the financial and economic downturn in 2008 owing to perceived risks and regulatory uncertainty in a volatile business world. According to Figure 2, experts expect a global upswing in FDI flows up to approximately $ 2 trillion by the end of 2014. In this example, FDI inflows to Financial Services are about 25% of total global services (UNCTAD, 2012). Furthermore, as depicted in Figure 3, FDI inflows to Financial Services exceeded those to the field of Manufacturing. This result is in line with Pain's (1989) findings because the manufacturing share has decreased meanwhile that of financial services expanded. As presented in Table 1, the UK has been selected for the most promising investor for attracting FDI in 2011. This phenomenon confirms Zschiedrich's (2004) view because a robust and stable economy enhances and favors the inward FDI in one industrial area. This explains the top position of London as the capital of the UK in 2011 in Table 2. The next part discovers in more depth the main incentives with some incoherent exemplary FDI determinants by shifting from the macro to micro point of view.

2.) FDI from a Micro Perspective

According to the IMF (2012), the determinants of inward FDI are interdependent and mutually influence each other. The most crucial incentive is to maintain ownership of at least 10% in the foreign venture along with the greater opportunity to respond to local services and products. (OECD, 2012). In accordance with Porter's (1998) and Krugman's et al. (2011) theory of an international and competitive cluster, foreign firms mainly engaged in FDI projects in cluster regions because they underscore proximity, similarity and market participant linkage. Following this idea, Zschiedrich (2006) introduces some attributes of a modern globalisation cluster which consists of aggregated demand and internal infrastructure.[1] Porter (1998) and Kutschker et al. (2008) contradict Cernavin (2005) because it is generally accepted that the state does have an essential impact on the development of a cluster.[2] Pursuant to a questionnaire conducted by FDI Intelligence in 2008, some judging criteria include economic potential, business friendliness and quality of life and are thus classified in Zschiedrich's (2006) and Porter (1998) quality assessment of a cluster. Based on the above explained cluster theory, the following part defines and evaluates some inward FDI determinants.

3.) A Technical Model of FDI

The model shown in Table 3 and developed below examines six exemplary and random determinants of the ultimate FDI (Y_t) decision of a global company to the financial service cluster in

---

[1] National and regional demand equals Gross Domestic Product (GDP) and Gross Value Added (GVA) respectively. Internal infrastructure is related to trade and is measured in the Balance of Payment (BoP) and the Net trade difference.

[2] The state grants tax incentives and contributes to social security.

London. In other words, it is to investigate whether they led to the inward FDI flow. The parameters belonging to the *demand* attribute are GDP of the UK in $ million (X_1) and Gross Value Added in Financial Services in the UK in $ million (X_4). The factor *internal infrastructure* comprises the determinants Balance of Payment of the UK in $ million (X_2) and Net Trade in the UK in $ million (X_3). The criterion *state* includes the independent variables Corporate Tax Rate in % (X_5) and Employer Social Security Contribution Rate in % (X_6).[3] Therefore, the pre-analytical economic model looks as follows:

$$Y_t = \alpha + \beta_1 X_{1t} + \beta_2 X_{2t} + \beta_3 X_{3t} + \beta_4 X_{4t} + \beta_5 X_{5t} + \beta_6 X_{6t} + \varepsilon_t \qquad (1)$$

The following section focuses on the classical regression model A, B and C assumptions (Brand, 2012). The first assumption (A1) is to prove ''the exogenity of all six relevant regressors and that no used variable is irrelevant'' using the Ordinary Least Square (OLS) method[4]. It is important to remember

---

[3] The model is set within a static framework and for simplification dynamic adjustments are hold constant.

[4] Schulze et al., (2012) provide a detailed way of calculating a ''K-dimensional'' regression equation pp.134-139.

that they are still determinants even though they are randomly taken from a sample data set. (Wooldridge, 2007). After the testing of A1 has been run as shown in Table 4, the correct economic model is shown below:

$$Y_t = \alpha + \beta_3 X_{3t} + \beta_4 X_{4t} + \beta_6 X_{6t} + \varepsilon_t \qquad (2)$$

Equation number 39 is the correct sample regression model because it has the highest adjusted coefficient of determination R^2 with 0,371. In other words, the independent variables Net Trade in the UK in $ million (X_3), Gross Value Added in Financial Services in the UK in $ million (X_4) and Employer Social Security Contribution Rate in % (X_6) explain approximately 37% of the entire quadratic variation in FDI inwards flows (Y_t). However, this adjusted R^2 value and the error numbers imply that there may be omitted numbers or other random and predictable factors that have an influence on the inward FDI as shown in Table 5. It is reasonable to undertake further studies and researches for finding other independent variables, so that Y_t has a stronger linear relationship to them. Eventually, A1 is violated because variables X_1, X_2 and X_5 are ''missing exogenous variables and are irrelevant'' according to the results in Table 4.

After the correct model has been detected, the linear relationship between the relevant and independent variables Net Trade in the UK in $ million (X_3), Gross Value Added in Financial Services in the UK in $ million (X_4), Employer Social Security Contribution Rate in % (X_6) and the dependent variable Y (FDI Inwards Flow) is to be detected. According to the results in Table 6, the second assumption (A2) is violated which is also emphasized in Graphs 1a – c. The linear relationship between the scatter plots and the function are poorly positive. A further proof is given in Graphs 2a – c. Pursuant to their statistical movements[5], they are not normally distributed as shown in Diagrams 1a – c. The null hypothesis is rejected and the alternative hypothesis is applied. Therefore, referring back to Table 6, the variable X_3 and X_6 best fit a logarithmic model (Graph 3a - b) and X_4 a log inverse model (Graph 3c). In comparison to the latter Diagrams 1a - c, the corrected Diagrams 2a - c approximately follow an estimated normal distribution. The transformations are:

---

[5] If the independent variables are linearly related to the dependent variable, they should graphically follow a standard normal distribution where the mean, skewness and kurtosis are 0 and the variance is 1.

For X3: ln ŷ (x3)= a + b3*ln x3 => ŷ (x3)= e^a * e^(b3 ln x3) with **y= e^u** and ln x3= $\tilde{x}_3$

$$\hat{u}(x3) = a + b3 * \tilde{x}_3 \qquad (3)$$

For X4: ln ŷ (x4)= a + b4*1/x4 => ŷ (x4)= e^a * e^(b4*1/x4) with **y=e^r** and 1/x4= $\tilde{x}_4$

$$\hat{r}(x4) = a + b4 * \tilde{x}_4 \qquad (4)$$

For X6: ln ŷ (x6)= a + b6*ln x6 => ŷ (x6)= e^a * e^(b6 ln x6) with **y= e^j** and ln x6= $\tilde{x}_6$

$$\hat{j}(x6) = a + b6 * \tilde{x}_6 \qquad (5)$$

After the variables have been transformed back, the final linear equation looks as follows:

$$\hat{y}_t = a + b3\, \tilde{x}_{3t} + b4\, \tilde{x}_{4t} + b6\, \tilde{x}_{6t} + e_t \qquad (6)$$

After a regression analysis for equation 6 has been performed, the optimized adjusted R^2 is 0,425 compared with 0,371. Also, the errors are smaller when comparing Diagram 3 and 4. With this equation A3 is violated. For X3, major structural breaks are shown in Graphs 3a-b:

Period I → between interval 2 and 7 (1986-1991): $\hat{y}_t =$ $a_1 + b_{31}\, \tilde{x}_{3t} + \varepsilon_t$ \qquad (7)

Period II → between interval 14 and 16 (1998 – 2000):
$$\hat{y}_t = a_{II} + b_{3II}\tilde{x}_{3t} + \varepsilon_t \tag{8}$$
Period III → after interval 22 (2006 – beyond): $\hat{y}_t = a_{III} + b_{3III}\tilde{x}_{3t} + \varepsilon_t$ \hfill (9)

A possible re-specification of the economic model for the sum of all three periods is:

For Period I + II (1986-2000) $a_{II} = a_I + \gamma_1$ ^ $b_{II} = b_I + \delta_1$ \hfill (10)

For Period II + III (1992-2006) $a_{III} = a_{II} + \gamma_2$ ^ $b_{III} = b_{II} + \delta_2$ \hfill (11)

Rewriting the equation for X3 results in: $\hat{y}_t = a_I + \gamma_1 + \gamma_2 + b_I\tilde{x}_3 + \delta_1\tilde{x}_3 + \delta_2\tilde{x}_3 + \varepsilon_t$ \hfill (12)

For X4, major structural breaks are as shown in Graphs 4a-b:

Period I → between interval 1 and 6 (1985 – 1990): $\hat{y}_t = a_I + b_{4I}\tilde{x}_{4t} + \varepsilon_t$ \hfill (13)

Period II → between interval 7 and 11 (1991-1998):
$$\hat{y}_t = a_{II} + b_{4II}\tilde{x}_{4t} + \varepsilon_t \tag{14}$$

Period III → between interval 12 and 17 (1996 – 2001): $\hat{y}_t = a_{III} + b_{4III}\tilde{x}_{4t} + \varepsilon_t$ \hfill (15)

Period IV → after interval 22 (2006 – beyond): $\hat{y}_t = a_{IV} + b_{4IV}\tilde{x}_{4t} + \varepsilon_t$ \hfill (16)

A possible re-specification of the economic model for the sum of all four periods is:

For Period I + II (1985-1998) $a_{II} = a_I + \gamma_1$ ^ $b_{II} = b_I + \delta_1$ (17)

For Period II + III (1991-2001) $a_{III} = a_{II} + \gamma_2$ ^ $b_{III} = b_{II} + \delta_2$ (18)

For Period III + IV (1996 – 2006) $a_{IV} = a_{III} + \gamma_3$ ^ $b_{IV} = b_{III} + \delta_3$ (19)

Rewriting the equation for X4 results in:

$$\hat{y}_t = a_I + \gamma_1 + \gamma_2 + \gamma_3 + b_I \tilde{x}_4 + \delta_1 \tilde{x}_4 + \delta_2 \tilde{x}_4 + \delta_3 \tilde{x}_4 + \varepsilon_t \quad (20)$$

For X6, major structural breaks are as shown in Graphs 5a-b:

Period I → between interval 1 and 5 (1985 – 1989): $\hat{y}_t = a_I + b_{4I} \tilde{x}_{6t} + \varepsilon_t$ (21)

Period II → between interval 5 and 8 (1989 – 1992): $\hat{y}_t = a_{II} + b_{4II} \tilde{x}_{6t} + \varepsilon_t$ (22)

A possible re-specification of the economic model for the sum of all four periods is:

For Period I + II (1985-1992) $a_{II} = a_I + \gamma_1$ ^ $b_{II} = b_I + \delta_1$ (23)

Rewriting the equation for X4 results in: $\hat{y}_t = a_I + \gamma_1 + b_I \tilde{x}_6 + \delta_1 \tilde{x}_6 + \varepsilon_t$ (24)

The reasons for the structural break, partially derived from Figure 1, are, for instance, financial and economic booms and downturns like during the collapse of the Soviet Union in 1991, the speculative ''dot-com bubble'' in the late 90s and the banking and sovereign debt crisis in 2007/08. Eventually, all alphas and betas are not constant for all 26 observations. Reflecting on the B1 Assumption and based on the results from A1 and A2, it is concluded from Table 7 and 8 that, though ''corrected'', the expected error variable E (ϵ_t) is not zero for the optimal model from A2 for all 26 observations. Hence B1 is violated because in our model the residuals depend on the regressors. In this regard, for the variables X_3, X_4 and X_6, all residuals have a different distance below and above the function as shown in Graphs 1 - 2a – c. Consequently, assumptions B2 and 3 are violated because the error variance σ^2, given the explanatory variables, is not constant. As the variance depends on the residuals, heteroskedacticity is present as shown in Graphs 2a – c and in Table 10. The latter phenomena suggest that the residuals for the best equation from A1 and A2 are not normally distributed which violates assumption B4. This scenario for the economic model from A1 and A2 are depicted in Diagram 3 and 4 respectively. For the final C2 Assumption, there is no perfect multicolinearity for all 26 observations amongst the relevant variables X_3, X_4 and X_6 as shown in Table 9. However, in Table 10, a positive and negative tendency for correlation between the variables can be detected which results in multicolinerarity. This dilemma can be sold through collecting more sample data. In conclusion, the variance inflation factor (VIF) is below 10 and hence, multicolinearity does not pose a problem of estimating $β_3$, $β_4$ and $β_6$. This section specified an economic model according to its functions (A – Assumptions), noise variables (B – Assumptions) and independent variables (C – Assumption). (Brand, 2012).

III. Conclusion and outlook

Based on the results from the former section, the question of how much exemplary FDI determinants according to FDI Intelligence 2008 and Table 5 impacts the FDI inflow in the financial service sector in London is difficult to answer and needs evaluating in the following years. To go a step further, public and private investment could be analyzed in regards to employment, transportation and infrastructure projects, productivity, household income and sustainable business creation. In this context, it is worth to study to which extent FDI inward flows have an impact on regional disparities and development in the UK.

VI. Appendix

VI.1　Figures
VI.2　Tables
VI.3　Graphs
VI.4　Diagrams

VI.1 Figures

Figure 1

Global FDI Inflows by Group of Economies between 1995 and 2011 (in $ Billion)

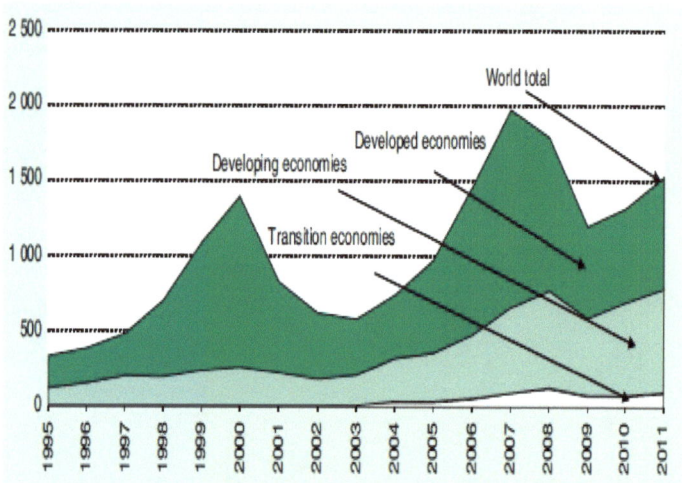

Source: UNCTAD (2012).

Figure 2

Global FDI Flows between 2002 and 2011, and Projection for 2012 – 2014 (in $ Billion)

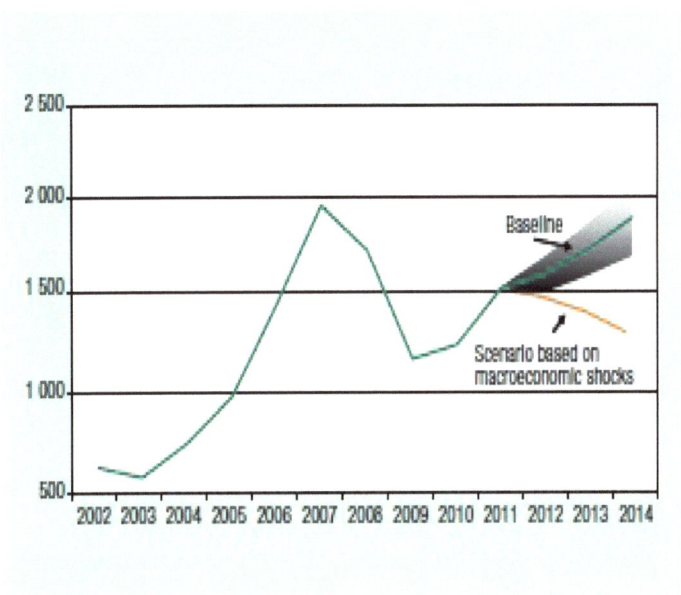

Source: UNCTAD (2012).

Figure 3

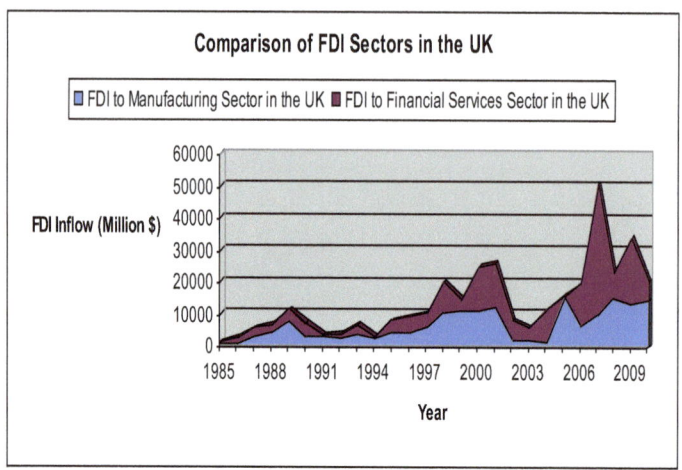

Source: Office for National Statistics (2012).

VI.2 Tables

Table 1

Top 10 Source Countries from Europe in 2011

Country	No of projects	% change
UK	1359	12%
Germany	1237	7%
France	647	3%
Spain	423	-0.9%
Switzerland	390	-12%
Netherlands	371	-4%
Italy	249	-0.7%
Sweden	237	-6%
Ireland	168	21%
Austria	166	-19%
Other	1010	0.08%
Total	**6383**	**2%**

Source: FDI Markets (2012).

Table 2

Top 10 Majors Cities according to Business Friendliness

RANK	CITY	COUNTRY
1	London	UK
2	Moscow	Russia
3	Brussels	Belgium
4	Warsaw	Poland
5	Prague	Czech Rep
6	Paris	France
7	Copenhagen	Denmark
8	Stockholm	Sweden
9	Bucharest	Romania
10	Dublin	Ireland

Source: FDI Intelligence (2012).

Table 3

Original Data Set for Analysis

Year	T	y	X1	X2	X3	X4	X5	X6
1985	1	83.00	464241.10	3314.27	-6622.97	252000.00	40	10.45
1986	2	1570.00	570434.70	-1323.75	2103.50	310763.50	35	10.45
1987	3	2567.00	705517.10	-12589.60	5056.16	385083.80	35	10.45
1988	4	2514.00	851183.60	-35326.20	26975.82	472661.20	35	10.45
1989	5	3772.00	859452.60	-43108.50	30855.43	483774.80	35	10.45
1990	6	4013.00	1013617.00	-38810.90	21421.30	585566.50	34	10.45
1991	7	526.00	1065816.00	-19021.90	6897.52	625349.90	33	10.40
1992	8	1400.00	1091801.00	-23204.20	11753.78	657432.40	33	10.40
1993	9	3225.00	981161.70	-17721.10	7337.01	597429.40	33	10.40
1994	10	430.00	1060543.00	-10025.80	4537.62	640581.50	33	10.20
1995	11	3750.00	1157177.00	-13436.40	1354.02	693071.00	33	10.20
1996	12	5046.00	1219621.00	-10328.60	-920.50	736670.40	33	10.20
1997	13	4523.00	1358815.00	-1402.65	-7183.60	832151.20	31	10.00
1998	14	9662.00	1455975.00	-5273.00	11380.81	910562.30	31	10.00
1999	15	3969.00	1502889.00	-3547.40	21672.76	950907.70	30	12.20
2000	16	13698.00	1477132.00	-38800.30	27260.04	937701.80	30	12.20
2001	17	13727.00	1470694.00	-30280.80	34509.22	951161.40	30	11.90
2002	18	6073.00	1617706.00	-27858.20	42015.92	1062796.00	30	11.80
2003	19	3998.00	1860395.00	-30002.00	42975.19	1245751.00	30	12.60
2004	20	10182.00	2201417.00	-45414.90	59766.01	1482238.00	30	12.60
2005	21	-28.00	2280538.00	-59406.00	77643.87	1540006.00	30	12.60
2006	22	13283.00	2444581.00	-81957.60	74943.88	1651952.00	30	12.80
2007	23	40696.00	2812877.00	-71079.40	85536.97	1910755.00	30	12.80
2008	24	7487.00	2639954.00	-41159.10	71923.58	1824705.00	28	12.80
2009	25	20616.00	2171385.00	-37050.50	39938.04	1529761.00	28	12.80
2010	26	5304.00	2253552.00	-75229.00	61318.40	1536898.00	28	12.80

Y1: Inward FDI flow in $ million
X1: GDP of the UK in $ million
X2: Balance of Payment of the UK in $ million
X3: Net Trade in the UK in $ million
X4: Gross Value Added in Financial Services in the UK in $ million
X5: Corporate Tax Rate in %
X6: Employer Social Security Contribution Rate in %

Source: Own composition and accessed through OECD (2012), UNCTAD (2012), EuroStat (2012) and Office for National Statistics in the UK (2012).

Table 4

Results from Assumption A1

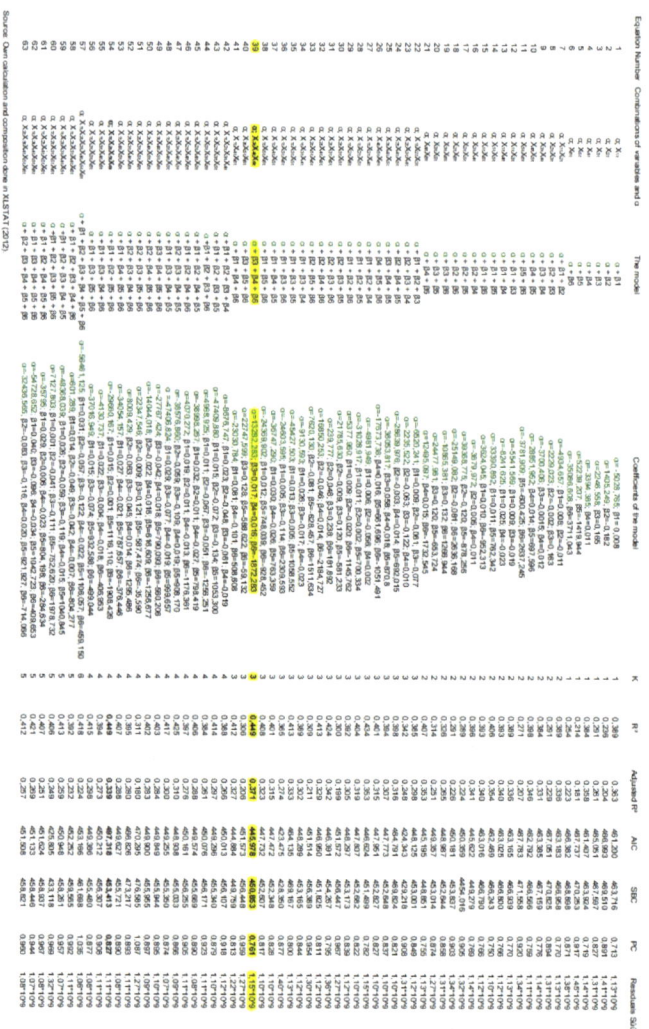

Table 5

Assessment of Cluster Quality

Attribute	Hard Parameter	Soft Parameter
Labour	Labour Force	Knowledge
Transport Infrastructure	Transport Network	Efficiency
Major Participants	Original Equipment Manufacturer	Domestically and globally integrated value chain
Direct Internal Infrastructure	Related and supported industries Suppliers	Innovation Strategic partnerships Knowledge transfer
Indirect Internal Infrastructure	R&D institutions Universities	Knowledge Experience
Demand	Market size	Quality
State	Incentives	Cluster policy

Source: Zschiedrich (2006).

Table 6

Results from Assumption A2

Variable	Testing Model	R^2	Adjusted R^2	Mean	Variance	Skewness	Kurtosis
X_3	Linear Lin	0,291	0,261	7019,462	73717704,4	2,45	6,689
	Semilogarithmic	0,21	0,172	7515,391	80865658	2,273	5,568
	Quadratic	0,006	-0,035	7019,462	73717704,4	2,45	6,689
	Inverse	0,312	0,283	7019,462	73717704,4	2,45	6,689
	Exponential	0,336	0,306	8825	1,73	-0,955	1,171
	Logarithmic	**0,434**	**0,406**	**8444**	**1235**	**-0,298**	**-0,307**
	Log Inverse	0,009	-0,034	8285	1730	-0,955	1,171
X_4	Linear Lin	0,384	0,358	7019,462	73717704,4	2,45	6,689
	Semilogarithmic	0,32	0,292	7019,462	73717704,4	2,45	6,689
	Quadratic	0,224	0,192	7019,462	73717704,4	2,45	6,689
	Inverse	0,418	0,394	7019,462	73717704,4	2,45	6,689
	Exponential	0,494	0,471	8285	1,73	-0,955	1,171
	Logarithmic	0,572	0,553	8285	1730	-0,955	1,171
	Log Inverse	**0,582**	**0,564**	**8285**	**1730**	**-0,955**	**1,171**
X_6	Linear Lin	0,254	0,223	7019,462	73717704,4	2,45	6,689
	Semilogarithmic	0,251	0,22	7019,462	73717704,4	2,45	6,689
	Quadratic	0,248	0,217	7019,462	73717704,4	2,45	6,689
	Inverse	0,257	0,226	7019,462	73717704,4	2,45	6,689
	Exponential	0,256	0,225	7019,462	73717704,4	2,45	6,689
	Logarithmic	**0,344**	**0,316**	**8285**	**1730**	**-0,955**	**1,171**
	Log Inverse	0,34	0,311	8285	1730	-0,955	1,171

Source: Own calculation and composition in XLSTAT (2012).

Table 7

Results from Assumption B1 for the Best Model from A1

Predictions and residuals:

Observation	Weight	y	Pred(y)	Residual	Std. residual	Adjusted Pred	Sûû
Obs1	1	83,000	-2454,194	2537,194	0,365	-3018,097	6437351,895
Obs2	1	1570,000	-1387,739	2957,739	0,425	-1872,914	8748222,537
Obs3	1	2567,000	-175,094	2742,094	0,394	-511,374	7519078,215
Obs4	1	2514,000	1569,337	944,663	0,136	1304,329	892388,1343
Obs5	1	3772,000	1809,490	1962,510	0,282	1097,648	3851444,068
Obs6	1	4013,000	3241,352	771,648	0,111	3144,757	595441,1691
Obs7	1	526,000	3707,015	-3181,015	-0,458	3935,383	10118855,82
Obs8	1	1400,000	4291,763	-2891,763	-0,416	4500,066	8362294,314
Obs9	1	3225,000	3277,946	-52,946	-0,008	3281,655	2803,325743
Obs10	1	430,000	4279,272	-3849,272	-0,554	4652,703	14816893,37
Obs11	1	3750,000	5045,575	-1295,575	-0,186	5213,547	1678513,79
Obs12	1	5046,000	5688,417	-642,417	-0,092	5799,535	412700,0846
Obs13	1	4523,000	7448,739	-2925,739	-0,421	8687,013	8559949,101
Obs14	1	9662,000	8992,437	669,563	0,096	8774,365	448314,8244
Obs15	1	3989,000	5680,362	-1691,362	-0,243	6126,468	2860705,114
Obs16	1	13898,000	5569,451	8328,549	1,198	3890,173	69364730,57
Obs17	1	13727,000	6465,619	7261,381	1,045	5851,886	52727647,63
Obs18	1	6073,000	8526,880	-2453,880	-0,353	8676,460	6021526,14
Obs19	1	3998,000	9531,839	-5533,839	-0,796	10680,810	30623370,87
Obs20	1	10182,000	13516,995	-3334,995	-0,480	13941,538	11122191,72
Obs21	1	-28,000	14726,155	-14754,155	-2,122	18429,056	217685099
Obs22	1	13283,000	16430,441	-3147,441	-0,453	17111,955	9906385,249
Obs23	1	40896,000	20655,096	20240,904	2,912	10521,368	409694192,4
Obs25	1	20616,000	13920,886	6695,114	0,963	11707,211	44824545,02
Obs26	1	5304,000	14660,959	-9356,959	-1,346	15945,148	87552679,38
Obs24	1	7487,000	19080,074	-11593,074	-1,668	19080,074	134399359,8

Source: Own calculation XLSTAT (2012).

Table 8

Results from Assumption B1 for the Best Model from A2

Observation	Weight	ln y	Pred(ln y)	Residual	Std. residual	dev. on pred.	lv bound 95%	l' bound 95%	l on pred.	lObs und 95%	lObs und 95%	lObsAdjusted Pred	Súú
Obs2	1	7,358	7,012	0,346	0,403	0,422	6,121	7,903	0,958	4,992	9,033	7,080	0,12095096
Obs3	1	7,850	7,429	0,421	0,490	0,272	6,855	8,003	0,901	5,527	9,331	7,468	0,17746787
Obs4	1	7,830	8,024	-0,195	-0,226	0,221	7,557	8,491	0,887	6,152	9,897	8,038	0,037876
Obs5	1	8,235	8,075	0,161	0,187	0,245	7,558	8,591	0,894	6,189	9,960	8,061	0,02576412
Obs6	1	8,297	8,078	0,220	0,256	0,288	7,469	8,686	0,907	6,165	9,990	8,050	0,0492714
Obs7	1	6,265	7,781	-1,516	-1,764	0,229	7,298	8,264	0,889	5,905	9,658	7,897	2,2976002
Obs8	1	7,244	7,949	-0,705	-0,820	0,292	7,333	8,566	0,908	6,034	9,864	8,041	0,49682452
Obs9	1	8,079	7,777	0,302	0,351	0,216	7,321	8,233	0,886	5,907	9,646	7,756	0,09121536
Obs10	1	6,064	7,607	-1,543	-1,795	0,252	7,075	8,138	0,896	5,717	9,496	7,752	2,3800081
Obs11	1	8,230	7,310	0,920	1,070	0,115	7,068	7,551	0,867	5,480	9,139	7,293	0,84636603
Obs14	1	9,176	7,918	1,258	1,464	0,487	6,890	8,945	0,988	5,833	10,002	7,322	1,58343105
Obs15	1	8,291	8,833	-0,542	-0,630	0,257	8,290	9,376	0,897	6,940	10,726	8,898	0,29356298
Obs16	1	9,540	8,892	0,648	0,754	0,242	8,381	9,402	0,893	7,008	10,775	8,936	0,41976424
Obs17	1	9,527	8,869	0,658	0,765	0,167	8,517	9,222	0,876	7,022	10,717	8,844	0,43248823
Obs18	1	8,712	8,924	-0,212	-0,247	0,119	8,673	9,175	0,968	7,093	10,754	8,928	0,04509881
Obs19	1	8,294	9,267	-0,973	-1,132	0,269	8,699	9,834	0,901	7,366	11,167	9,372	0,94675969
Obs20	1	9,228	9,393	-0,165	-0,192	0,171	9,032	9,755	0,876	7,544	11,242	9,400	0,02710866
Obs22	1	9,494	9,475	0,019	0,022	0,054	9,361	9,588	0,861	7,658	11,292	9,475	0,00037368
Obs23	1	10,619	9,534	1,085	1,262	0,139	9,240	9,827	0,871	7,697	11,371	9,561	1,17720315
Obs25	1	9,934	9,289	0,645	0,750	0,229	8,806	9,772	0,889	7,413	11,165	9,240	0,41578103
Obs26	1	8,576	9,409	-0,833	-0,969	0,150	9,093	9,726	0,872	7,588	11,250	9,435	0,69373678
Obs24	1	8,921	9,480	-0,558	-0,651	0,063	9,347	9,613	0,857	7,672	11,286	9,480	0,31256686

The predictions and residuals corresponding to the observations of the validation set are displayed in the second part of the table

12,8694003

Source: Own calculation XLSTAT (2012).

Table 9

Multicolinearity Statistics

Multicolinearity statistics:

Statistic	ln X3	1/x4	ln X6
Tolerance	0,354	0,405	0,304
VIF	2,826	2,469	3,286

Source: Own calculation XLSTAT (2012).

Table 10

Correlation Matrix

Variables	ln X3	1/x4	ln X6	ln y
ln X3	**1,000**	-0,701	0,786	0,659
1/x4	-0,701	**1,000**	-0,750	-0,616
ln X6	0,786	-0,750	**1,000**	0,675
ln y	0,659	-0,616	0,675	**1,000**

Source: Own calculation XLSTAT (2012).

VI.3 Graphs

Graph 1a:

Relationship between X_3 and Y

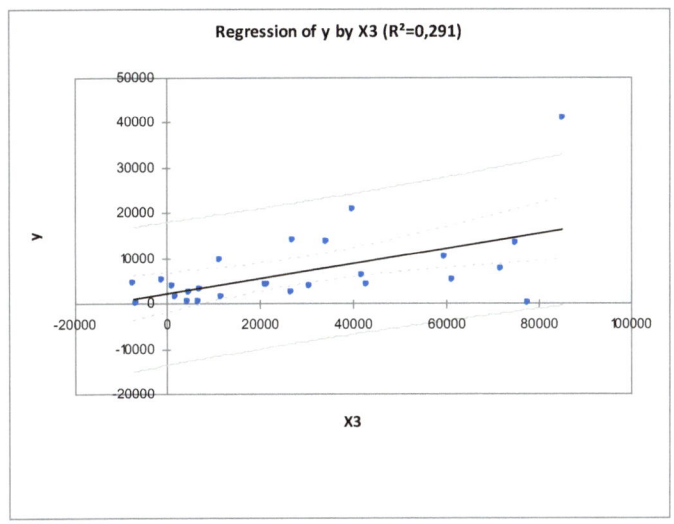

Source: Own calculation XLSTAT (2012).

Graph 1b:

Relationship between X_4 and Y

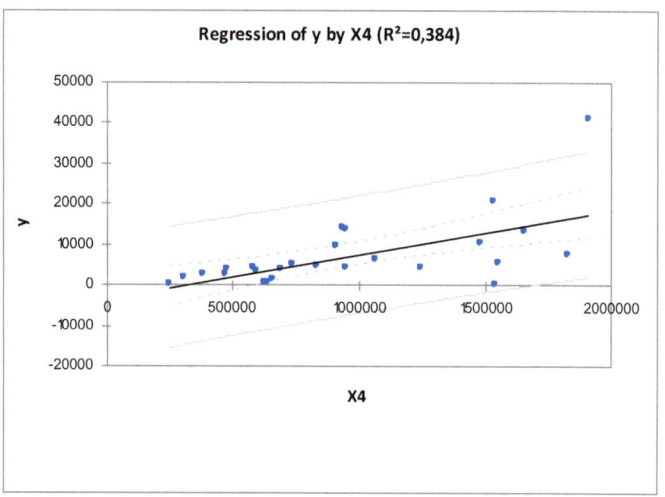

Source: Own calculation XLSTAT (2012).

Graph 1c:

Relationship between X_6 and Y

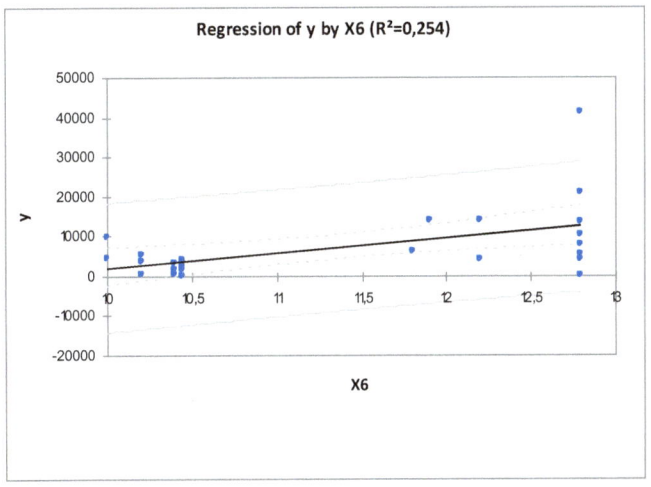

Source: Own calculation XLSTAT (2012).

Graph 2a:

Relationship between ln X₃ and ln Y

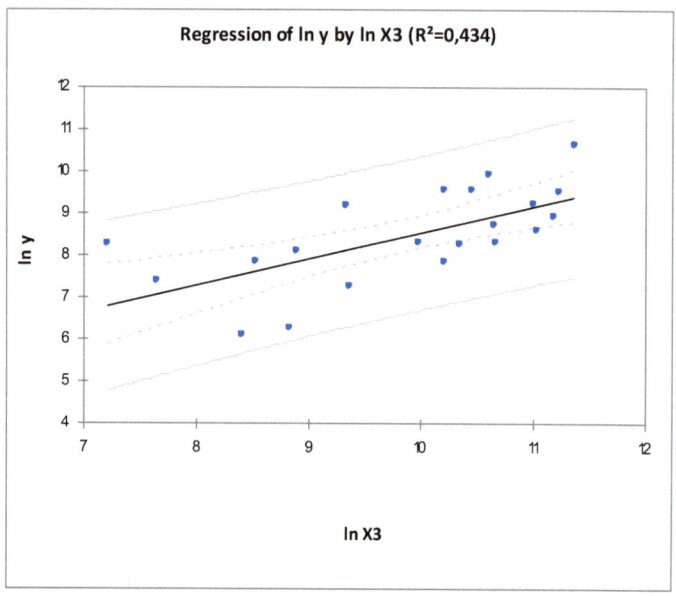

Source: Own calculation XLSTAT (2012).

Graph 2b:

Relationship between ln X_6 and ln Y

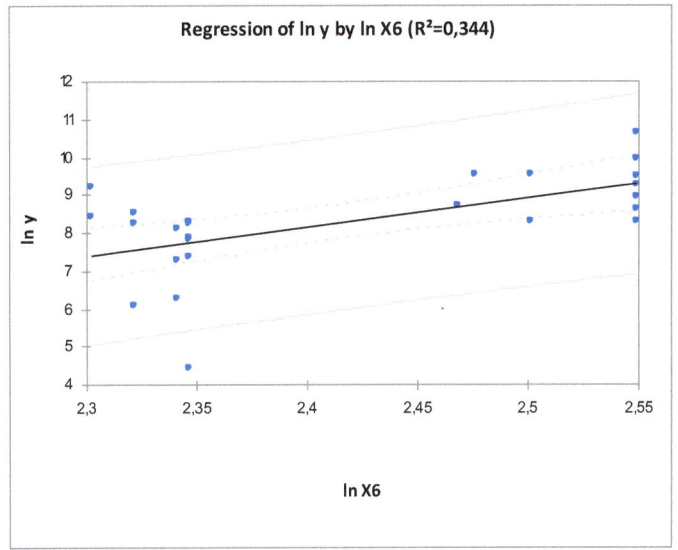

Source: Own calculation XLSTAT (2012).

Graph 2c:

Relationship between 1/X₄ and ln Y

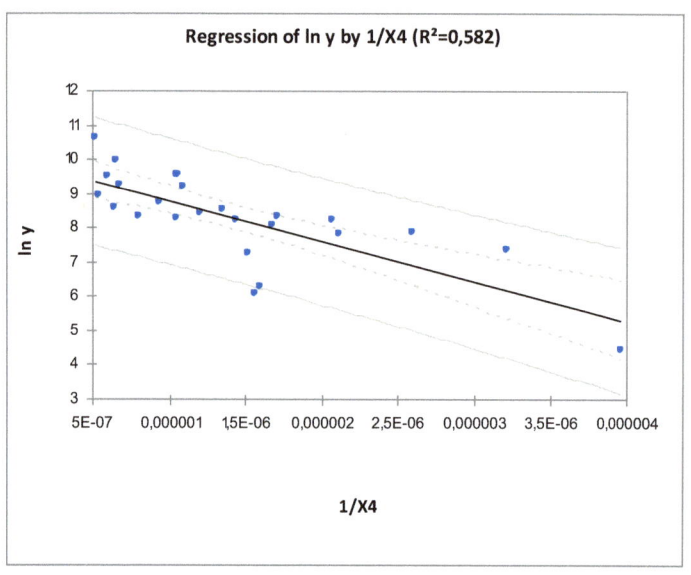

Source: Own calculation XLSTAT (2012).

Graph 3a:

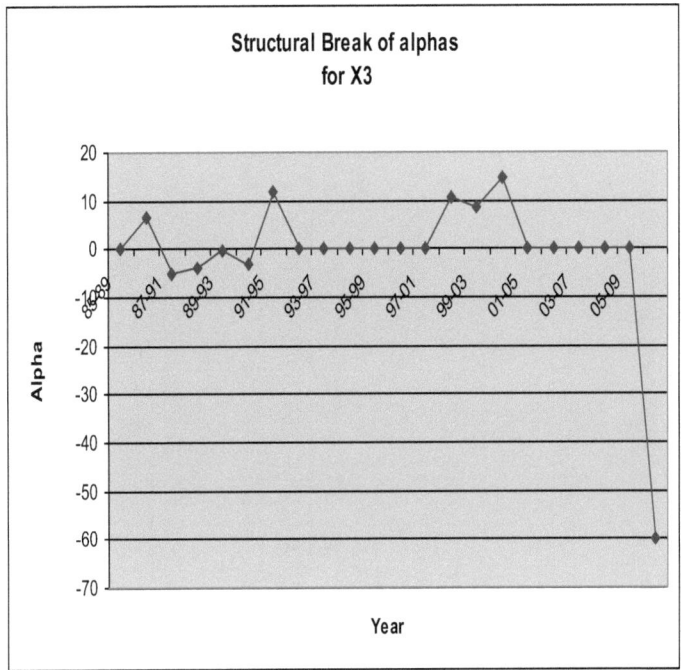

Source: Office for National Statistics (2012) and own calculation XLSTAT (2012).

Graph 3b:

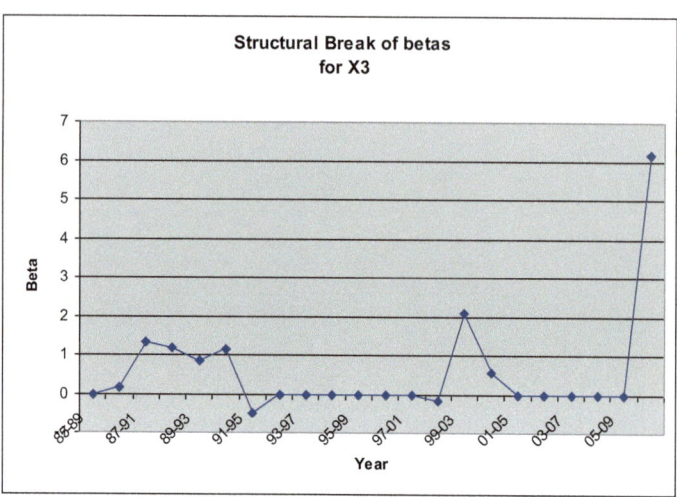

Source: Office for National Statistics (2012) and own calculation XLSTAT (2012).

Graph 4a:

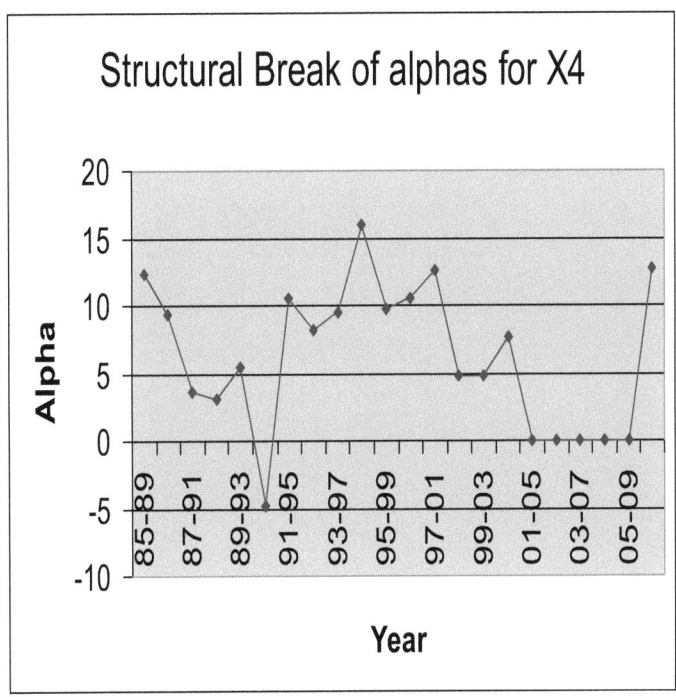

Source: Office for National Statistics (2012) and own calculation XLSTAT (2012).

Graph 4b:

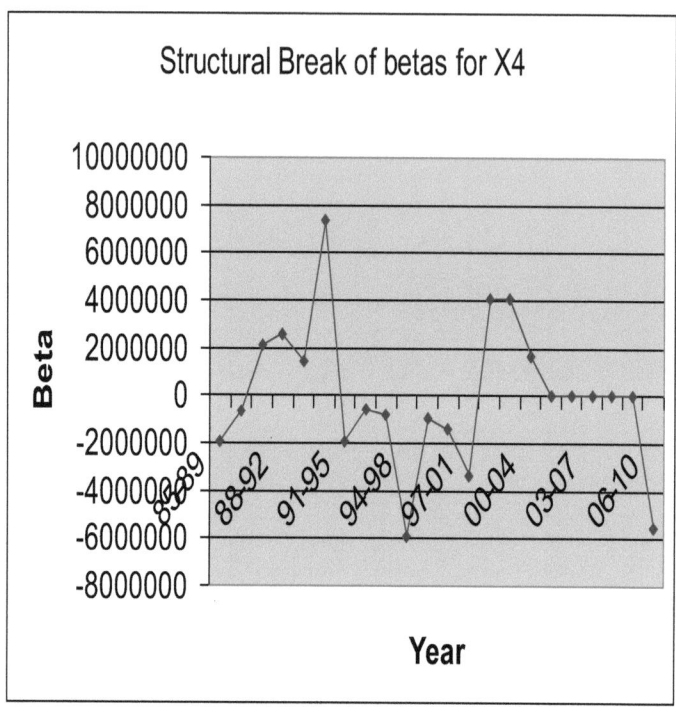

Source: Office for National Statistics (2012) and own calculation XLSTAT (2012).

Graph 5a:

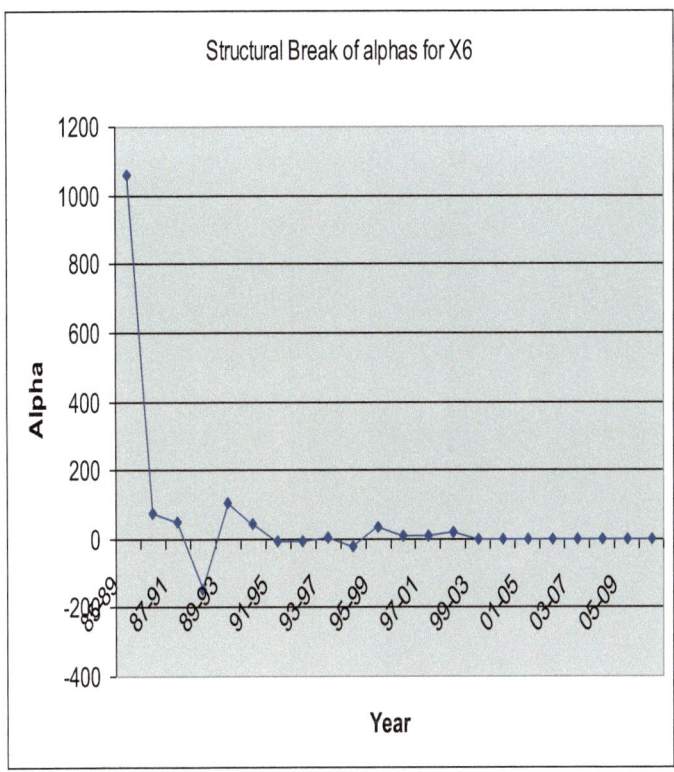

Source: Office for National Statistics (2012) and own calculation XLSTAT (2012).

Graph 5b:

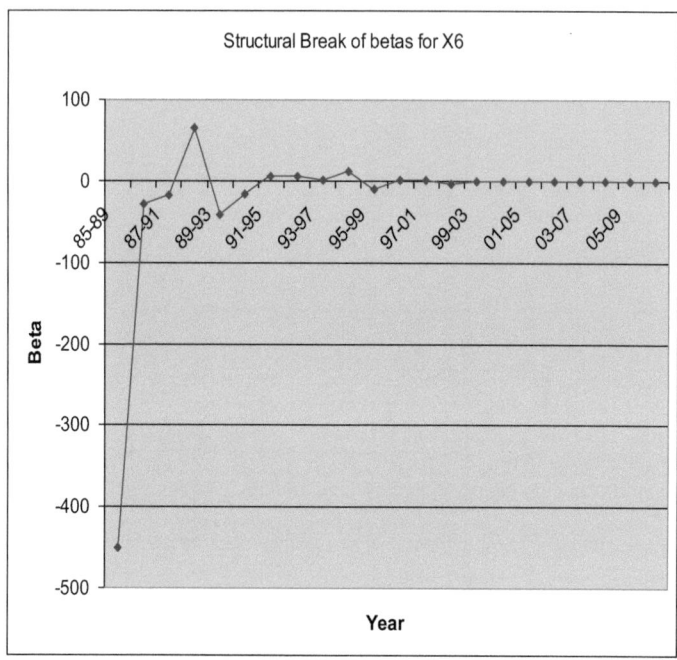

Source: Office for National Statistics (2012) and own calculation XLSTAT (2012).

VI.4 Diagrams

Diagram 1a:

Uncorrected Distribution for X_3

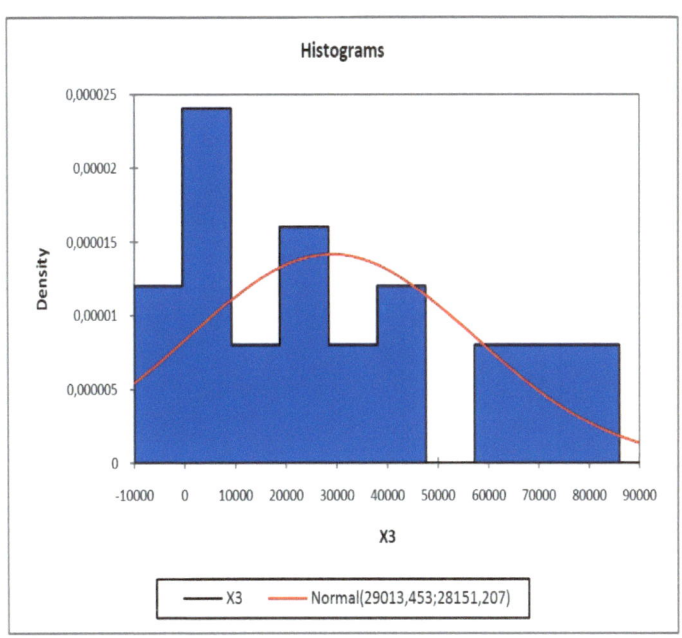

Source: Own calculation XLSTAT (2012).

Diagram 1b:

Uncorrected Distribution for X_4

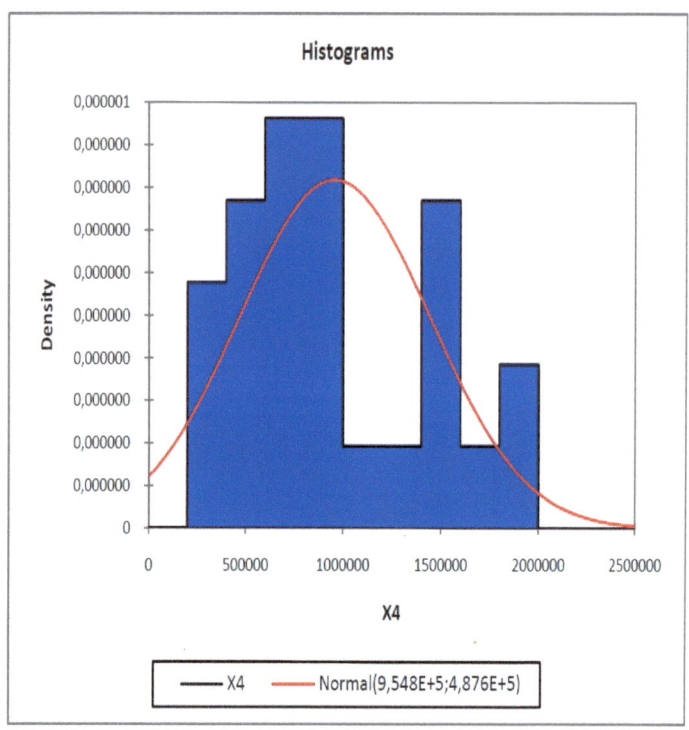

Source: Own calculation XLSTAT (2012).

Diagram 1c:

Uncorrected Distribution for X_6

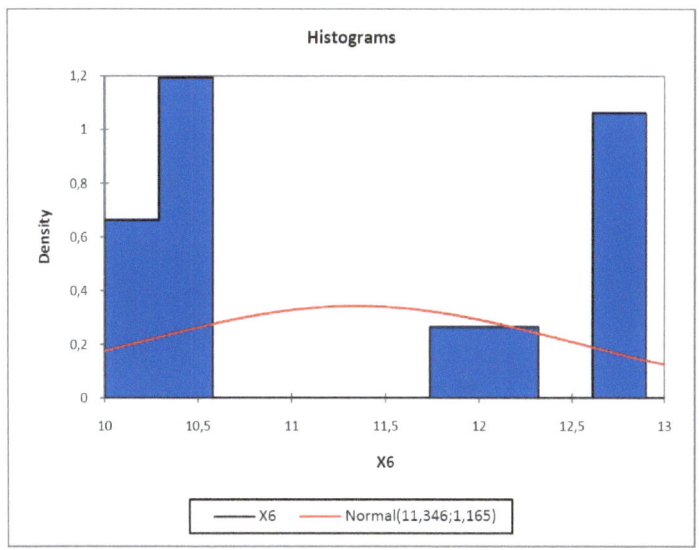

Source: Own calculation XLSTAT (2012).

Diagram 2a:

Corrected Distribution for X₃

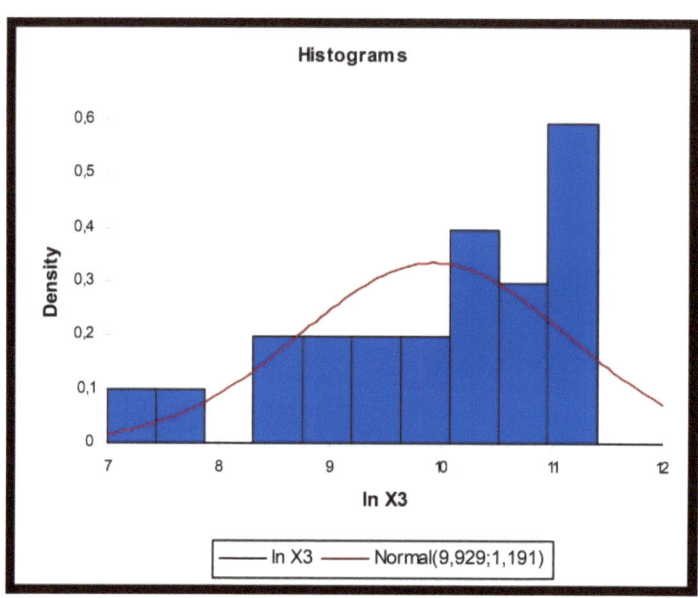

Source: Own calculation XLSTAT (2012).

Diagram 2b:

Corrected Distribution for X_4

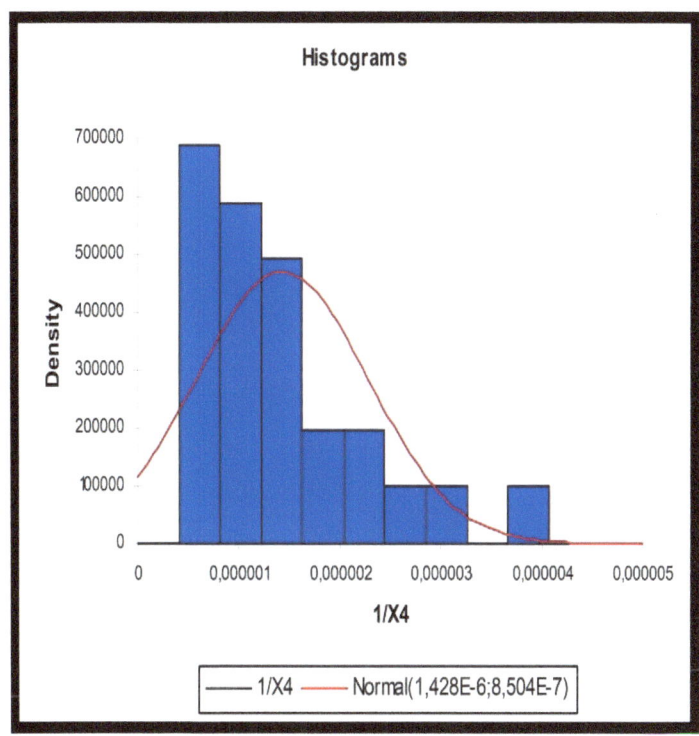

Source: Own calculation XLSTAT (2012).

Diagram 2c:

Corrected Distribution for X_6

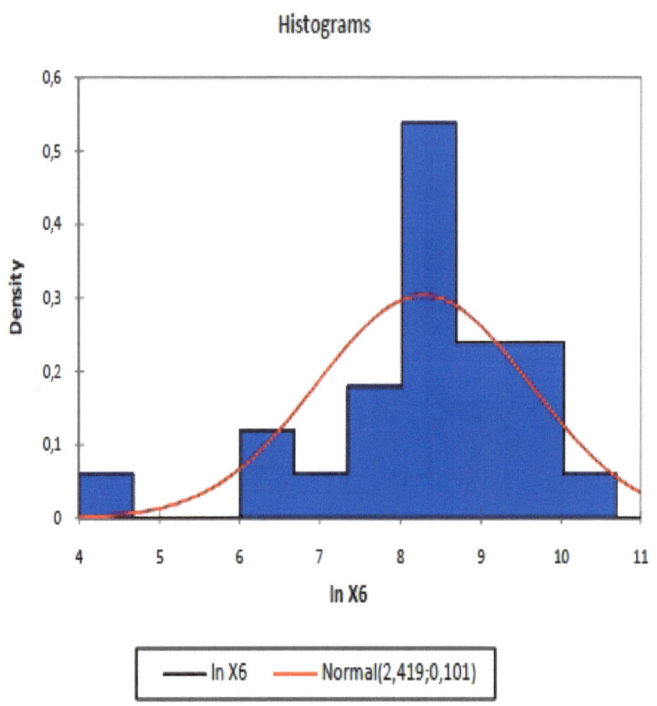

Source: Own calculation XLSTAT (2012).

Diagram 3:

Distribution of Residuals from the Best Model from A1

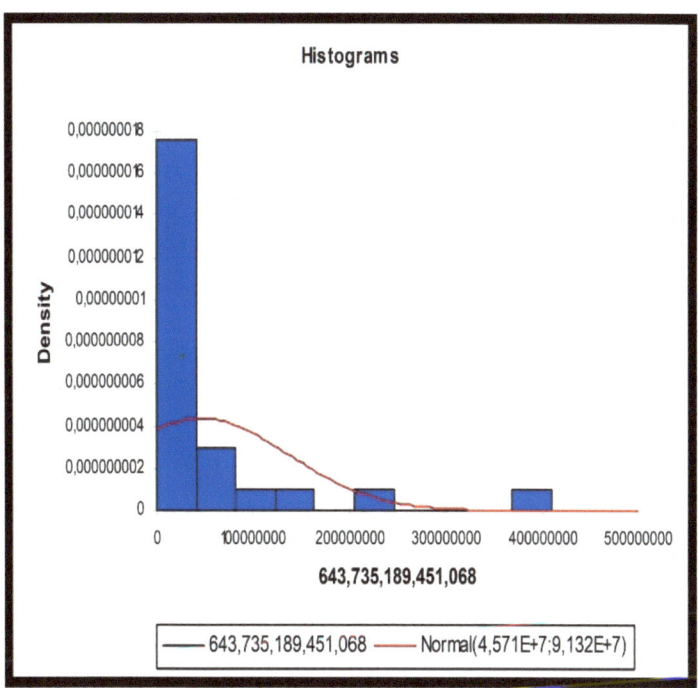

Source: Own calculation XLSTAT (2012).

Diagram 4:

Distribution of Residuals from the Best Model from A2

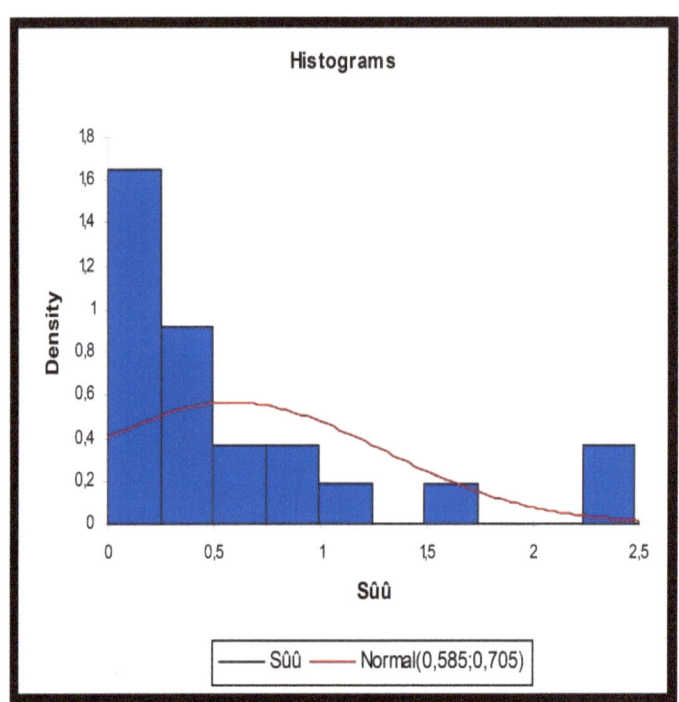

Source: Own calculation XLSTAT (2012).

V. References

Bradley, J. and and Fitzgerald, J., 1990, *Production structures in a small open economy with mobile and indigenous investment.* European Economic Review.

Brand, F., 2012, *Lectures in Econometrics.* Berlin: Hochschule für Wirtschaft und Recht.

Cernavin, O., 2005, *Regionale Cluster als soziale Innovationssysteme – Wandel der Arbeit und die wachsende Bedeutung der Cluster Perspektive,* in: *Cluster und Wettbewerbsfähigkeit von Regionen – Erfolgsfaktoren regionaler Wirtschaftsentwicklung.* Berlin: Duncker & Humblot GmbH.

FDI Intelligence (2012), *European Cities & Regions of the Future.* [Online]. Available at http://www.fdiintelligence.com [Accessed 20 November 2012].

IMF, 2012, *Foreign Direct Investment in Developed Market Countries.* [PDF]. Available at http://www.imf.org/external/np/cmcg/2003/eng/091803.pdf [Accessed 10 December 2012].

Krugman, P., Obstfeld, M. and Melitz, M., 2011, *International Economics – Theory and Policy.* Boston: Pearson Education Limited.

Kutschker, M. and Schmied, S., 2008, *Internationales Management.* Munich: Oldenburg Verlag.

OECD, 2008, *OECD Benchmark and Definition of Foreign Direct Investment.* [Online]. Available at http://www.oecd.org/dataoecd/26/50/40193734.pdf [Accessed 5 October 2012].

Pain, N.C.,1989, *International direct investment flows and the UK economy,* National Institute of Economic and Social Research.

Porter, M., 1998, *The Competitive Advantage of Nations.* London: McMillan.

Schulze, P. and Porath, D., 2012, *Statistik mit Datenanalyse und ökonometrischen Grundlagen.* Munich: Oldenburg Verlag.

UNCTAD, 2012, *World Investment Report 2012.* [PDF] Available at http://www.unctad-docs.org/files/UNCTAD-WIR2012-Full-en.pdf [Accessed 20 December 2012].

Wooldridge, J.M., 2007, *Introductory Econometrics.* Michigan State University.

Zschiedrich, H, 2004, *Internationales Management in den Märkten Mittel – und Osteuropas.* Munich: Rainer Hampp Verlag.

Zschiedrich, H, 2006, *Ausländische Direktinvestitionen und regionale Industriecluster in Mittel- und Osteuropa.* Munich: Rainer Hampp Verlag.

www.ingramcontent.com/pod-product-compliance
Lightning Source LLC
Chambersburg PA
CBHW040329220526
45473CB00009B/2617